SOCIAL PROGRESS AND SUSTAINABILITY

Shelter • Safety • Literacy • Health • Freedom • Environment

EAST ASIA AND THE PACIFIC

Foreword by **Michael Green,**
Executive Director, Social Progress Imperative

By Amy Hackney Blackwell

SOCIAL PROGRESS AND SUSTAINABILITY

THE SERIES:

AFRICA: NORTHERN AND EASTERN

AFRICA: MIDDLE, WESTERN, AND SOUTHERN

EAST ASIA AND THE PACIFIC

EUROPE

EURASIA

NEAR EAST

SOUTH AND CENTRAL ASIA

NORTH AMERICA

CENTRAL AMERICA AND THE CARIBBEAN

SOUTH AMERICA

SOCIAL PROGRESS AND SUSTAINABILITY

Shelter • Safety • Literacy • Health • Freedom • Environment

EAST ASIA AND THE PACIFIC

Amy Hackney Blackwell

Foreword by
Michael Green
Executive Director, Social Progress Imperative

MASON CREST

Mason Crest
450 Parkway Drive, Suite D
Broomall, PA 19008
www.masoncrest.com

Printed and bound in the United States of America

First printing
9 8 7 6 5 4 3 2 1

Series ISBN: 978-1-4222-3490-7
Hardcover ISBN: 978-1-4222-3494-5
ebook ISBN: 978-1-4222-8389-9

Library of Congress Cataloging-in-Publication Data

Names: Hackney Blackwell, Amy, author.
Title: East Asia and the Pacific/by Amy Hackney Blackwell; foreword by Michael Green, executive director, Social Progress Imperative.
Description: Broomall, PA : Mason Crest, [2017] | Series: Social progress and sustainability | Includes index.
Identifiers: LCCN 2016007603| ISBN 9781422234945 (hardback) | ISBN 9781422283899 (ebook)
Subjects: LCSH: Social accounting—Asia. | Social accounting—Pacific Area. | Quality of life—Asia. | Quality of life—Pacific Area. | Asia—Social conditions—21 century. | Pacific Area—Social conditions—21st century.
Classification: LCC HN652.7 .H33 2017 | DDC 306.095—dc23
LC record available at http://lccn.loc.gov/2016007603

Developed and Produced by Print Matters Productions, Inc. (www.printmattersinc.com)

Project Editor: David Andrews
Design: Bill Madrid, Madrid Design
Copy Editor: Laura Daly

CONTENTS

KEY ICONS TO LOOK FOR:

Text-Dependent Questions: These questions send readers back to the text for more careful attention to the evidence presented there.

Words to Understand: These words with their easy-to-understand definitions will increase readers' understanding of the text while building vocabulary skills.

Series Glossary of Key Terms: This back-of-the-book glossary contains terminology used throughout this series. Words found here increase readers' ability to read and comprehend higher-level books and articles in this field.

Research Projects: Readers are pointed toward areas of further inquiry connected to each chapter. Suggestions are provided for projects that encourage deeper research and analysis.

Sidebars: This boxed material within the main text allows readers to build knowledge, gain insights, explore possibilities, and broaden their perspectives by weaving together additional information to provide realistic and holistic perspectives.

SOCIAL PROGRESS AROUND THE GLOBE

Michael Green

How do you measure the success of a country? It's not as easy as you might think. Americans are used to thinking of their country as the best in the world, but what does "best" actually mean? For a long time, the United States performed better than any other country in terms of the sheer size of its economy, and bigger was considered better. Yet China caught up with the United States in 2014 and now has a larger overall economy.

What about average wealth? The United States does far better than China here but not as well as several countries in Europe and the Middle East.

Most of us would like to be richer, but is money really what we care about? Is wealth really how we want to measure the success of countries—or cities, neighborhoods, families, and individuals? Would you really want to be rich if it meant not having access to the World Wide Web, or suffering a painful disease, or not being safe when you walked near your home?

Using money to compare societies has a long history, including the invention in the 1930s of an economic measurement called gross domestic product (GDP). Basically, GDP for the United States "measures the output of goods and services produced by labor and property located within the U.S. during a given time period." The concept of GDP was actually created by the economist Simon Kuznets for use by the federal government. Using measures like GDP to guide national economic policies helped pull the United States out of the Great Depression and helped Europe and Japan recover after World War II. As they say in business school, if you can measure it, you can manage it.

Many positive activities contribute to GDP, such as
• Building schools and roads
• Growing crops and raising livestock
• Providing medical care

More and more experts, however, are seeing that we may need another way to measure the success of a nation.

Other kinds of activities increase a country's GDP, but are these signs that a country is moving in a positive direction?
• Building and maintaining larger prisons for more inmates
• Cleaning up after hurricanes or other natural disasters
• Buying alcohol and illegal drugs
• Maintaining ecologically unsustainable use of water, harvesting of trees, or catching of fish

GDP also does not address inequality. A few people could become extraordinarily wealthy, while the rest of a country is plunged into poverty and hunger, but this wouldn't be reflected in the GDP.

In the turbulent 1960s, Robert F. Kennedy, the attorney general of the United States and brother of President John F. Kennedy, famously said of GDP during a 1968 address to students at the University of Kansas: "It counts napalm and counts nuclear warheads and armored cars for the police to fight the riots in our cities ... [but] the gross national product does not allow for the health of our children.... [I]t measures everything in short, except that which makes life worthwhile."

For countries like the United States that already have large or strong economies, it is not clear that simply making the economy larger will improve human welfare. Developed countries struggle with issues like obesity, diabetes, crime, and environmental challenges. Increasingly, even poorer countries are struggling with these same issues.

Noting the difficulties that many countries experience as they grow wealthier (such as increased crime and obesity), people around the world have begun to wonder: What if we measure the things we really care about directly, rather than assuming that greater GDP will mean improvement in everything we care about? Is that even possible?

The good news is that it is. There is a new way to think about prosperity, one that does not depend on measuring economic activity using traditional tools like GDP.

Advocates of the "Beyond GDP" movement, people ranging from university professors to leaders of businesses, from politicians to religious leaders, are calling for more attention to directly measuring things we all care about, such as hunger, homelessness, disease, and unsafe water.

One of the new tools that have been developed is called the Social Progress Index (SPI), and it is the data from this index that is featured in this series of books, Social Progress and Sustainability.

The SPI has been created to measure and advance social progress outcomes at a fine level of detail in communities of different sizes and at different levels of wealth. This means that we can compare the performance of very different countries using one standard set of measurements, to get a sense of how well different countries perform compared to each other. The index measures how the different parts of society, including governments, businesses, not-for-profits, social entrepreneurs, universities, and colleges, work together to improve human welfare. Similarly, it does not strictly measure the actions taken in a particular place. Instead, it measures the outcomes in a place.

The SPI begins by defining what it means to be a good society, structured around three fundamental themes:

- Do people have the basic needs for survival: food, water, shelter, and safety?
- Do people have the building blocks of a better future: education, information, health, and sustainable ecosystems?

- Do people have a chance to fulfill their dreams and aspirations by having rights and freedom of choice, without discrimination, with access to the cutting edge of human knowledge?

The Social Progress Index is published each year, using the best available data for all the countries covered. You can explore the data on our website at http://socialprogressimperative. org. The data for this series of books is from our 2015 index, which covered 133 countries. Countries that do not appear in the 2015 index did not have the right data available to be included.

A few examples will help illustrate how overall Social Progress Index scores compare to measures of economic productivity (for example, GDP per capita), and also how countries can differ on specific lenses of social performance.

- The United States (6th for GDP per capita, 16th for SPI overall) ranks 6th for Shelter but 68th in Health and Wellness, because of factors such as obesity and death from heart disease.
- South Africa (62nd for GDP per capita, 63rd for SPI) ranks 44th in Access to Information and Communications but only 114th in Health and Wellness, because of factors such as relatively short life expectancy and obesity.
- India (93rd for GDP per capita, 101st for SPI) ranks 70th in Personal Rights but only 128th in Tolerance and Inclusion, because of factors such as low tolerance for different religions and low tolerance for homosexuals.
- China (66th for GDP per capita, 92nd for SPI) ranks 58th in Shelter but 84th in Water and Sanitation, because of factors such as access to piped water.
- Brazil (55th for GDP per capita, 42nd for SPI) ranks 61st in Nutrition and Basic Medical Care but only 122nd in Personal Safety, because of factors such as a high homicide rate.

The Social Progress Index focuses on outcomes. Politicians can boast that the government has spent millions on feeding the hungry; the SPI measures how well fed people really are. Businesses can boast investing money in their operations or how many hours their employees have volunteered in the community; the SPI measures actual literacy rates and access to the Internet. Legislators and administrators might focus on how much a country spends on health care; the SPI measures how long and how healthily people live. The index doesn't measure whether countries have passed laws against discrimination; it measures whether people experience discrimination. And so on.

- What if your family measured its success only by the amount of money it brought in but ignored the health and education of members of the family?
- What if a neighborhood focused only on the happiness of the majority while discriminating against one family because they were different?
- What if a country focused on building fast cars but was unable to provide clean water and air?

The Social Progress Index can also be adapted to measure human well-being in areas smaller than a whole country.

- A Social Progress Index for the Amazon region of Brazil, home to 24 million people and covering one of the world's most precious environmental assets, shows how 800 different municipalities compare. A map of that region shows where needs are greatest and is informing a development strategy for the region that balances the interests of people and the planet. Nonprofits, businesses, and governments in Brazil are now using this data to improve the lives of the people living in the Amazon region.
- The European Commission—the governmental body that manages the European Union—is using the Social Progress Index to compare the performance of multiple regions in each of 28 countries and to inform development strategies.
- We envision a future where the Social Progress Index will be used by communities of different sizes around the world to measure how well they are performing and to help guide governments, businesses, and nonprofits to make better choices about what they focus on improving, including learning lessons from other communities of similar size and wealth that may be performing better on some fronts. Even in the United States subnational social progress indexes are underway to help direct equitable growth for communities.

The Social Progress Index is intended to be used along with economic measurements such as GDP, which have been effective in guiding decisions that have lifted hundreds of millions of people out of abject poverty. But it is designed to let countries go even further, not just making economies larger but helping them devote resources to where they will improve social progress the most. The vision of my organization, the Social Progress Imperative, which created the Social Progress Index, is that in the future the Social Progress Index will be considered alongside GDP when people make decisions about how to invest money and time.

Imagine if we could measure what charities and volunteers really contribute to our societies. Imagine if businesses competed based on their whole contribution to society—not just economic, but social and environmental. Imagine if our politicians were held accountable for how much they made people's lives better, in real, tangible ways. Imagine if everyone, everywhere, woke up thinking about how their community performed on social progress and about what they could do to make it better.

Note on Text:
While Michael Green wrote the foreword and data is from the 2015 Social Progress Index, the rest of the text is not by Michael Green or the Social Progress Imperative.

This political map shows the countries of the region discussed in this book.

SOCIAL PROGRESS IN EAST ASIA AND THE PACIFIC

*S*ocial progress is a society's ability to meet the basic human needs of its citizens, to create the building blocks that individuals and communities use to improve the quality of their lives, and to make it possible for them to reach their potential. This is not the same thing as economic prosperity, which is limited to money and profits and can give misleading impressions of a society's actual conditions. While development includes economic factors, social progress considers the many other things that affect quality of life, some of which can make life good even if a strict economic definition would suggest otherwise.

The Social Progress Imperative measures various aspects of social progress in every country in the world for which data is available. The data comes from international organizations such as the World Bank, the World Health Organization, and the United Nations. The Imperative uses this information to create its Social Progress Index (SPI), which scores nations on how well they perform in three categories:

Basic Human Needs: *Does a country provide for its people's most essential needs?*

Foundations of Well-being: *Are the building blocks in place for individuals and communities to enhance and sustain well-being?*

Opportunity: *Is there opportunity for all individuals to reach their full potential?*

The SPI ranks countries from best to worst and arranges them in six groups ranging from very high to very low social progress. SPI rankings cover

133 countries, with 1 the best and 133 the worst. Many other nations are unranked but appear in the Social Progress Imperative's reports.

East Asia Pacific is a very large region and includes very different countries. China is a massive nation with a large population and thousands of years of recorded history and culture. Land-locked Mongolia is in the process of transforming from a nomadic society into a more urban, modern one. Japan was an economic powerhouse in the late 20th century and is still one of the most technologically advanced nations in the world. South Korea is nearly as economically prosperous as Japan, but North Korea has been closed to most commerce and communication with the rest of the world since its founding in 1948 and as a result is extremely poor. The nations of Southeast Asia still suffer from the aftereffects of wars that raged for decades and subsequent political instability; AIDS is also a serious problem throughout this region. Australia and New Zealand were settled by British colonists in the 18th and 19th centuries and thus are inhabited largely by English-speaking people of European ancestry. The island nations that dot the Pacific all have cultures of their own; the vast distances that separate them from one another and the mainland make all types of communication and transportation difficult.

As you might expect, these countries show a wide range of social progress. New Zealand earned an overall rank of 5th in the world, Australia ranks 10th, Japan 15th, and South Korea 29th. On the other end, Myanmar ranks 119th overall, close to the bottom of the 133 ranked nations. Cambodia is 99th and Laos 102nd. Thailand, Malaysia, and the Philippines sit in the middle. The Social Progress Imperative could not gather enough information on North Korea, Papua New Guinea, or Vietnam to create a full score, although it is likely that the first two scores would have been quite low, and Vietnam's would have been in the moderate low category. Singapore and Taiwan also lack scores, which would likely have been high.

The entire region has fairly strong scores in the category of Health and Wellness, and Japan has the longest life expectancy in the world. Japan also scores high in Personal Rights. On the other hand, repressive regimes in China, Vietnam, Laos, and Myanmar (formerly known as Burma) give those nations very low scores in Personal Rights. Mongolia has high scores in Opportunity, especially in Personal Rights. New Zealand and Australia stand out in all areas, with some of the highest social progress scores in the world.

Vietnamese military mine sweepers scan for unexploded ordnance left over from the Vietnam War during a US government–funded program. In the four decades since the war ended, an estimated 42,000 people have been killed or injured by mines and other explosives.

BASIC HUMAN NEEDS

Do you have enough food to eat? Is it nutritious? Can you drink the water that comes out of your sink? Do you even have a sink? What about a toilet? Do you have a home that you can sleep in every day? Can you go places without being attacked?

Basic human needs are things people need in order to be healthy and comfortable. In the United States, most, but certainly not all, people have access to enough food, clean water, clean toilets, and comfortable homes. Most of us feel that we can walk the streets or drive our cars without worrying about criminal attacks, though there are certainly unsafe areas.

Our level of comfort is not universal. In the East Asia Pacific region, some countries meet basic human needs at least as well as the United States, whereas others fare much worse. Within the region, Japan scores the highest, 95.01, putting it in 5th place worldwide. Timor-Leste, fresh from years of a war for independence, scores the lowest, 50.55. Korea, Singapore, New Zealand, Thailand, and Australia score well above the world average. Nations such as Myanmar, Laos, and Cambodia score below average.

A Laotian woman washes her clothes in the Mekong River, Southeast Asia's longest river.

Nutrition and Basic Medical Care

Nutrition and basic medical care are cornerstones of well-being. Without enough food, people starve. Without good nutrition, they are susceptible to diseases. Basic medical care includes treatment of the most fundamental and typical conditions, such as pregnancy and childhood diseases.

Enough to eat

Imagine that most of your food was just rice, with some vegetables and very occasionally meat or eggs. Some days there would be no food for lunch or dinner. You would be quite thin and probably not as tall as you are now. Think how hard it would be to concentrate on schoolwork if you were hungry all the time. This was the daily reality for many people in the East Asia Pacific region in the 20th century.

Over the past couple of decades, however, the nations of this region have made considerable improvement in meeting daily nutritional needs. According to the United Nations Food and Agriculture Organization (FAO), every nation in this region except Timor-Leste and North Korea has met the goal of halving the number of people suffering from malnourishment as of 1990.

That does not mean that malnutrition has been eradicated. Although people are better fed today than they used to be, there are still many who do not get enough calories every day. In Timor-Leste about 45 percent of children under five are underweight. In China 9.3 percent of people are undernourished. The figure rises to 20.5 percent in Mongolia, where one of every five people do not have enough food to meet daily minimum energy requirements. Malnutrition still exists throughout Southeast Asia.

North Korea's Famines

Malnourished children sleep on the floor in a kindergarten in a rural cooperative 300 kilometers (186 miles) from the capital Pyongyang. Born of mothers suffering during the national famine in 1998, these six-year-olds are only the size of properly nourished three- to four-year-olds and due to lack of strength sleep three to four hours each afternoon.

You may think of famine as a thing of the past, but in North Korea people starve to death on a regular basis. During the 1990s the nation suffered a severe famine. The loss of aid from the Soviet Union and China harmed the already shaky agricultural sector, and severe storms and floods destroyed almost all of the nation's crops and grain reserves. The totalitarian government refused to import food, so many people had nothing to eat. The estimates of deaths range widely depending on the source, but somewhere between 300,000 and 3 million people are believed to have died of starvation in the 1990s. Pregnant women suffered miscarriages. Children's growth was stunted. People survived by smuggling and black market trading or by sneaking across the border to China; those who were caught were sent to prison camps. Conditions since then have gone up and down, but periodic famines continue to occur.

Medical care

For the most part, basic medical care is good in the East Asia Pacific region, particularly in Australia, New Zealand, Japan, South Korea, and Singapore. Medical care is so good in the highest-scoring countries that **maternal mortality rates** (deaths of mothers during pregnancy or childbirth per 100,000 live births) and **child mortality rates** (deaths of children under the age of five per 1,000 live births) are very low.

Other nations do not do so well. Cambodia's child mortality rate is 51.36, making it the 36th worst in the world. The rate in Laos is even worse, 54.53. This is partly the result of a serious AIDS epidemic in Southeast Asia, which increases infant mortality rates. Poor nutrition does not help; some 29 percent of Cambodian children under the age of five are underweight. Infectious diseases are also a serious problem. On the other hand, the Social Progress Imperative points out that Cambodia's child mortality rate is better than that in many countries with a similar **GDP per capita**, such as Afghanistan, Bangladesh, and many sub-Saharan African nations.

Water and Sanitation

If you've ever been camping or hiking, you might have had to go to the bathroom in the woods. Before you drank water you took from a stream, you boiled it or used a water purifier. Bathing was difficult or impossible. It was probably a relief to get back home to your sink, shower, and toilet.

Can you drink the water?

For many people in the East Asia Pacific region, daily life is like camping. They do not have flushing toilets, sinks, or showers. The lack of clean water and sanitation puts people at serious risk of diseases such as typhoid, polio, dysentery, and cholera, all of which can spread when human feces end up in drinking water. Travelers to Southeast Asia are warned never to drink the water that comes out of sinks; that's asking for an upset stomach. Drinking water is boiled and kept in a special container for easy use; people do not drink water from the tap.

The Social Progress Imperative rates countries on what percentage of the population has water piped into their houses or yards and access to "improved sanitation," which means flush toilets with sewage systems or composting toilets. Clean water and flushing toilets are the rule in Singapore, Australia, New Zealand, and Japan. In other parts of the region, they are definitely the exception. In rural parts of Thailand, the customary bathing method is to dip water from a cistern with a bowl and pour it over oneself as sort of a handmade shower. Many toilets cannot handle toilet paper, so people place it in a trash can after use instead of flushing it away.

Shelter

At the end of a long day, nothing feels as good as going home—back to your own space, with your own things, where you can be comfortable. But what if you didn't have a home? Or what if that home was crowded, cold, hot, noisy, dark, or otherwise made it hard to relax?

Where to Go . . .

Papua New Guinea has a particularly low score in the category of Water and Sanitation. This is due largely to a pervasive custom known as "open defecation," that is, pooping behind bushes. Very few rural villages have toilets of any kind. Children defecate on the ground and then step in the feces, tracking them back into their houses. Defecating near rivers and streams spreads diseases because feces can easily wash into the water that people downstream use for drinking, and most Papuans still scoop their drinking water from streams and ponds. Hundreds of children die every year from diarrhea that they catch from contaminated water.

New Guinea is one of the least-urbanized countries in the world; only 13 percent of the population lives in cities, and 4 percent of city dwellers still practice open defecation. In 2015 only 9 percent of houses had piped water, and 19 percent had improved sanitation. Most people live much as their ancestors did in New Guinea's mountainous, heavily forested terrain. It is not easy to install plumbing in these areas, but the biggest challenge is getting people to change their behavior. Building latrines works only if people use them, and customs are hard to change.

Aboriginal at Goroka Tribal Festival, Papua New Guinea.

The types of shelter range widely in the East Asia Pacific region. Electricity and indoor plumbing are more common than they used to be, but there are still places that do not have them. There are also many places with completely modern dwellings. In Australia and New Zealand people live in houses much like those in American suburbs. Hong Kong is a very modern city. But in rural areas, shelter has not changed much since the last century. For example, the Dayak people of Borneo continue to live in traditional longhouses, large, multifamily houses in the jungle. The hill tribes of northern Thailand live in wooden dwellings without running water, although they are beginning to add electricity—sometimes from solar panels.

Dayak longhouse village in Borneo, Indonesia.

People in Japan have modern houses that are quite comfortable but that can be extremely small. Rents in Tokyo are so high that many people can only afford apartments that they jokingly call "rabbit hutches." This works because a single room can be used for multiple purposes. People sleep on futons, thick mats that they lay on the floors at night and put back in closets in the morning. That way, a single room can function as a living room/dining room during the day and a bedroom for an entire family at night.

Urban camping in Ulaanbaatar

Mongolia's low scores on shelter come partly from the problem of its capital city, Ulaanbaatar. The Mongolian people are traditionally nomadic, roaming the

Traditional ger huts used by Mongolian nomads.

steppes with their herds of animals. They live in tents called gers, or yurts, and cook on wood- or coal-burning stoves.

Harsh winters in recent years have devastated livestock and forced nomads to move to the city with their gers. Ulaanbaatar is now surrounded by massive suburbs of gers, which house more than half of the city's residents. These ger districts do not have running water or electricity. The air quality is terrible because all the residents still use their stoves, which produce massive amounts of smoke. There are no toilets. Winter temperatures can reach –31° Fahrenheit (–35° Celsius), which makes outdoor latrines even more unpleasant. Residents find it very hard to get work. The government and World Bank are working on the problem, but it will be extremely expensive to provide modern housing for everyone.

Personal Safety

When you leave your house to go to school or to go shopping, do you worry about being attacked? Do you know anyone who has been hit by a car? Have any of your friends' parents been arrested and imprisoned for their political beliefs? In much of the East Asia Pacific region, violent crime, traffic fatalities, and political terror are uncommon, but in some places they are an everyday concern, and personal safety is not something people take for granted.

Crime

East Asia has its share of crime, but there is a considerable range throughout the region. Japan has so little crime that people often leave empty, unlocked cars running in parking lots. If you forget your wallet in a store, it will almost certainly be there waiting for you when you return.

On the opposite ends of the spectrum are places like Port Moresby in Papua New Guinea, with one of the highest crime rates in the world, and the Malaysian capital Kuala Lumpur, which has recently gained a reputation for being one of the more crime-ridden cities in East Asia. In the 2000s and 2010s, residents of Kuala Lumpur were convinced that crimes were surging as gangs committed burglaries of homes, thefts of bags from pedestrians,

Traffic on Thanon Ratchadamri near Central World Plaza in central Bangkok,
a city infamous for its traffic jams.

and even murders. Drive-by thefts in which motorbike drivers snatch purses and backpacks are common. Although some experts dispute that crime has actually increased, numerous homeowners have paid to build gates to their communities, and business owners hire their own security guards to protect their properties.

Terrible traffic

Traffic in East Asia is a problem. During the first years of the 21st century, the number of cars on the roads everywhere skyrocketed. Cities such as Jakarta and Surabaya in Indonesia and Bangkok, Thailand, are notorious for some of the worst traffic in the world. (It can take five hours to drive from Bangkok's airport to its city center.) Other cities such as Tokyo, Beijing, and Hong Kong also have awful traffic. Not only does the time in traffic and accompanying pollution make life less pleasant, but the traffic is dangerous. In some nations traffic rules appear to be suggestions rather than requirements, police don't enforce the laws, and accidents are common.

Making matters worse, motorbikes are ubiquitous. In places like Saigon they are used as family vehicles, with mother, father, child, and baby all on one small scooter. Motorbike accidents can be painful if not fatal, but people keep riding the bikes because they are cheap and easily maneuverable in heavy traffic.

Text-Dependent Questions

1. What are basic human needs?
2. What kind of houses do Mongolian nomads live in?
3. Name some cities with terrible traffic.

Research Projects

Why are development agencies so concerned about clean water? What can contaminated water do to people? Investigate waterborne diseases and steps that societies can take to prevent illnesses from spreading through water.

CHAPTER 2

FOUNDATIONS OF WELL-BEING

Words to Understand

Biodiversity: the variety of plant and animal life in an area.

Carbon dioxide (CO_2): a greenhouse gas that contributes to global warming and climate change.

Ecosystem sustainability: when we care for resources like clean air, water, plants, and animals so that they will be available to future generations.

Greenhouse gases: gases that trap heat in the earth's atmosphere.

Infectious diseases: diseases caused by organisms, such as bacteria, viruses, fungi, or parasites. Some organisms are normally harmless or even helpful, but under certain conditions, they cause diseases that can be passed from person to person.

Literate: able to read.

Press: in journalism, the news media companies and those who work for them.

Well-being: the feeling people have when they are healthy, comfortable, and happy.

The foundations of **well-being** are things that make life good: wellness, education, access to information, and a clean, healthy environment. The Social Progress Imperative assesses foundations of well-being by looking at four categories:

- **Access to basic knowledge:** *Can children go to school? Can adults read and write?*
- **Access to information and communication:** *Do people have Internet and cell phones? Are they free to disagree with those in power?*
- **Health and wellness:** *How long do people live? Do they die early from treatable diseases?*
- **Ecosystem sustainability:** *Will future generations have a healthy environment in which to live?*

Most of the nations of the East Asia Pacific region have fairly good foundations of well-being but with plenty of room for improvement.

Access to Basic Knowledge

If you are reading this, you are literate. Don't take that for granted; many people are not. The SPI considers the ability to read part of access to basic knowledge. So is enrollment in school at various levels and equal rates of male and female school attendance. The SPI ranks Japan first in the world when it comes to access to basic knowledge. New Zealand is number three. South Korea is not far behind, at 16, and Australia is 29th. In all of these countries almost all children go to school at least into their early teens, girls as well as boys. Nearly all adults can read.

Education rates determine what sort of jobs people can do, which determines how they live and how much a nation's economy can grow. Educating girls improves a nation's economy by increasing the number of skilled workers and also by improving overall family health. But it is hard to persuade people that education is valuable when the rewards do not appear for years. Many families want their older children to work, especially the girls.

With support from international aid organizations, a school named New Bridge for Cambodia offers poor students free lessons on fundamental curriculums.

In 105th-ranked Cambodia, the overall literacy rate is 77 percent, and only 70 percent for girls and women. In the past decade some 1.3 million children were working in addition to or instead of going to school. In Laos (106th) in 2006, about 11 percent of children ages 5 to 14 were working. About 27 percent of women and 13 percent of men were illiterate. In Papua New Guinea some rural children never attend school at all.

Timor-Leste, one of the world's newest nations, has struggled with education since independence in 2002. Between 85 and 90 percent of the nation's schools were destroyed in the fighting that led up to independence, and the population has grown rapidly, creating more students in need of education. The government has had to act quickly to build schools and hire teachers, but it struggles to meet demand. As of the 2010s, the nation suffered from high adult illiteracy and low success at teaching children to read. Only about 37 percent of students make it to secondary school. UNICEF, UNESCO, and the World Bank were all contributing money to Timor-Leste's educational infrastructure in an effort to help the new country get on its feet.

Students listen to their teacher during a class at an elementary school in Likisa, Timor-Leste. The Southeast Asian island nation has a population of 1.2 million people, 40 percent of whom live in poverty.

Hard and Easy Languages

Once you learned to read, you could read anything written in English, even if you didn't understand it well. That is because English is written in an alphabet; all of our words can be expressed in combinations of just 26 characters, easily mastered by five-year-olds. Learn how to string letters together and sound out words, and you are off and running. But that is not the case with every language. Some are easy, and some are extraordinarily difficult.

Bahasa Indonesia, the Indonesian language, is considered easy to learn; it has no tenses, no genders, and has simple grammar. The Korean script, Hangul, consists of 24 characters that reflect the shape of the lips and tongue in speech; it is considered so easy to learn that people who speak other languages, such as the Cia-Cia language on the Indonesian island of Buton, have adopted it as their written alphabet.

Mandarin Chinese, on the other hand, is incredibly difficult to read and write and fairly hard to learn to speak. The spoken language uses tones to change meanings of sounds, and the written language consists of many thousands of complex characters. Japanese does not have tones, but its written form combines Chinese characters with two different "alphabets" that consist of syllables such as *ka* and *to*. The same Chinese character can be pronounced in different ways depending on how it is used in a word or sentence. It takes years to learn to read and write Chinese and Japanese, and many native speakers never fully master them.

Access to Information and Communications

In the United States we are accustomed to being able to access the Internet and communicate with people anywhere and at any time. Our many news sources cover thousands of stories every day, asking hard questions and getting answers. Several countries in the East Asia Pacific region have access to information and **press** freedom as good as or better than ours. New Zealand is the standout here, ranked number 8 on the SPI. Japan, Korea, and Australia are also strong in this area.

But access to information is not the rule. Myanmar is near the bottom of the world at number 131, below African nations such as Ethiopia and Chad. Laos is a dismal 128. China is ranked 105th, Cambodia 100th, and Indonesia 90th. Internet access in those countries is rare and uneven, hampered by spotty electricity. In 2014 Myanmar had only one fixed telephone line (landline) per 100 inhabitants. It did, however, have 48 cellular telephone subscriptions per 100 people, which was a significant improvement over previous years.

As Chinese citizens, workers at a wireless earphone factory in Shenzhen, China, face impeded access to information and communications.

Some East Asian governments control all media, which means that local people see and hear only what the government wants them to know. The Chinese Communist party owns all broadcast media outlets and dictates all programming; foreign shows must be approved by the government before they are shown, which means they often are not.

Until very recently, the people of Myanmar had almost no way to learn what was happening in the wider world. The government and army controlled the limited television and radio broadcasting available in the country. What

Pacific Island Internet

Pacific islands may be beautiful and romantic, but don't visit them expecting a good Internet connection. Where the Internet exists at all it is painfully slow. Emails and texts can take minutes or hours to go through, and that terrible service can be very expensive.

The reason is simple: the islands are spread hundreds or thousands of miles apart across the Pacific Ocean. Tonga, for example, consists of 52 islands dispersed over an area the size of Texas and only 105,000 inhabitants. Internet signals cross oceans on fiber-optic cables laid along the seafloor. Laying these cables is difficult even in areas with large populations to pay for the investment. In the Pacific, islands are so far apart and populations so small that telecommunications companies simply cannot afford to build cable systems. The island inhabitants are forced to rely on expensive and sporadic satellite signals.

The World Bank and local island governments are investing millions of dollars in cable networks in the hope of transforming island economies with high-speed Internet service. UNESCO has found that every 10 percent increase in an area's broadband access adds 1.4 percent to economic growth—very important for a largely agricultural rural country such as Tonga.

world news enters the country arrived as shortwave broadcasts such as Voice of America and satellite radio programs. Since 2012, however, journalists have been agitating for press freedom, government censorship has decreased, and people have been able to access more websites than in the past. Improvements have been real, but still most people have almost no access to real information, both because they cannot afford to pay for Internet or satellite radio, and because the government still exerts a heavy hand over media broadcasting.

Health and Wellness

The category of Health and Wellness goes beyond basic medical care to cover aspects of health that determine quality of life: life expectancy, premature

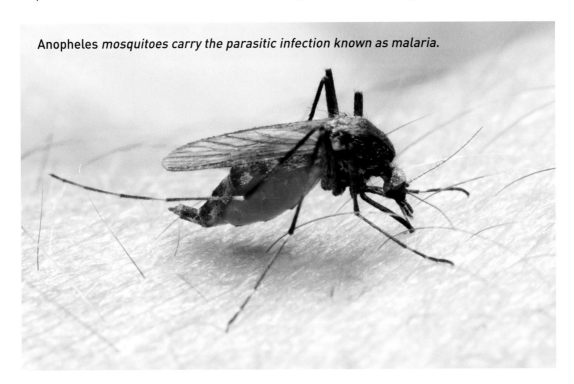

Anopheles *mosquitoes carry the parasitic infection known as malaria.*

deaths, obesity, suicide rates, and deaths caused by air pollution. Although Australia, New Zealand, Japan, and South Korea have excellent scores in this category (Japan has the highest life expectancy in the world: 84 years), there are some serious problems in much of the East Asia Pacific region.

Infectious diseases are found throughout the tropical parts of East Asia and the Pacific islands. Even when infectious diseases do not kill people, they can take them out of the workforce for weeks or months, hurting the economy. Common infectious diseases include hepatitis, typhoid, and diarrhea caused

Dutch Dr. Margareet Trip (right) examines a young woman who has malaria at the SMRU clinic in the Maela (also spelled Mae La) refugee camp north of Mae Sot, Thailand. The female patient is 18 years old and pregnant, so she gets extra attention because malaria can complicate a pregnancy.

by bacteria in food and water, as well as mosquito-transmitted malaria and dengue fever. In Cambodia, Laos, Myanmar, Thailand, and Vietnam, strains of malaria have appeared that are resistant to the drugs used to treat it. Dengue fever cannot be prevented by medicines. The best protection for both of these diseases is insect repellents, although a vaccine against malaria may soon be available.

Air pollution

Generally, air pollution in East Asia is terrible. The economies in this region are growing rapidly, which increases the number of cars and trucks on the

Beijing has an alarming level of air pollution. Sources include exhaust emission from Beijing's more than five million motor vehicles, coal burning, dust storms from the north, and local construction dust.

road, leading to greater pollution. In cities such as Jakarta and Beijing, the air quality is so bad that people wear face masks to walk around outside. The pollution makes people sick, cases of asthma and lung cancer are on the rise, and millions of children miss school every year due to illness caused by the air they breathe. China's health and wellness rank is a terrible 103, partly the result of deaths caused by air pollution. (China also has high rates of obesity and suicide.)

Forest fires cause a great deal of pollution. This problem is particularly severe in Indonesia, Singapore, Malaysia, and Thailand. Palm oil farmers in Indonesia set fires to forests to clear them for agriculture. The fires then

Indonesian soldiers spray water in a burned area of forest at Rimbo Panjang Village. During Indonesia's annual dry season, hundreds of fires are often illegally ignited to clear forests in the islands of Sumatra and Kalimantan, where large forest concessions are used by pulp and paper and palm oil companies.

spread to highly flammable peatlands and burn out of control for weeks. The resulting smoke spreads throughout the region, clouding the air in cities such as Singapore, far from farmers' fields. The haze grounds flights, closes schools, and sends thousands to the hospital with respiratory ailments and allergies. Arguments rage over who is responsible for the nearly annual blazes and accompanying pollution. Singapore's government wants Indonesia's palm oil industry to change its practices, but as of 2015 there was no solution in sight.

AIDS

Southeast Asia had one of the worst AIDS epidemics in the world during the 1990s. As of 2015 the HIV prevalence rate was still fairly high, especially in Indonesia (14th in the world based on number of people infected with HIV), Thailand (18th), Vietnam (22nd), Myanmar (27th), and Cambodia (49th). AIDS lowers life expectancy, causes higher infant mortality, and kills enough people to force population numbers lower than would otherwise be expected.

Several factors make AIDS a particular problem in this region. There are many intravenous drug users, and the use of sterile needles is uncommon. The many sex workers, including men who have sex with men, do not regularly use condoms. Education about the disease is uneven; many Thai sex workers have never been tested for HIV, and at least half of the population of Papua New Guinea has never even heard of AIDS. The stigma associated with HIV prevents people from revealing their status to sexual partners or family members who could support them, which both increases transmission of the virus and prevents patients from seeking treatment.

Ecosystem Sustainability

Most of the nations in the East Asia Pacific region get moderate to low scores on ecosystem sustainability. This is due to their rapid modernization: as nations increase education and economic opportunities, more people buy cars, more wild land is developed, and the worse off the environment becomes. Ironically, undeveloped Laos and Cambodia have very high scores for ecosystem sustainability, with high levels of untouched habitat and biodiversity.

Several East Asia Pacific nations are considered megabiodiverse, which means they have exceptionally high levels of **biodiversity**, with large numbers of species. Megabiodiverse nations in the East Asia Pacific region include China, Indonesia, Malaysia, Papua New Guinea, and the Philippines.

All of the Philippines' ecosystems are in decline. Between 2000 and 2005 the Philippines lost forests at a rapid rate, the result of commercial forestry and people cutting down trees to build houses and grow crops. Saltwater and freshwater bodies are polluted, destroyed, and converted to fisheries. At least 700 species of plants and animals are threatened or endangered. The Philippines is attempting to head off complete ecological destruction by passing laws requiring plans for development and protection of endangered species, but it faces an uphill battle against a growing population and economic development.

Megabiodiversity in the Philippines

The Philippines is a biodiversity hot spot, home to a vast number of plant and animal species; scientists discover new species every year. Between 70 and 80 percent of the world's plant and animal species are found there, including one of the world's smallest primates (the Philippine tarsier), biggest fish (the whale shark), and biggest moths (the Atlas moth). Almost a quarter of the nation's land is covered with forest ecosystems, home to thousands of species of birds. More than 3,000 species of fish live in its waters. These ecosystems help sustain human life and agriculture throughout the nation.

A Philippine child gets friendly with a tarsier—a tiny primate.

Samuel (l) and his father Phillip (r) search for useful items in what remained of their family home in Port Vila, capital of Vanuatu, after the worst tropical cyclone on record in the South Pacific. Global warming and rising seas pose a terrible threat to small island nations.

Global climate change is a particular concern for Pacific islands because it causes a phenomenon they can neither deny nor ignore: rising sea levels that swamp their low-lying land. The Pacific island nations Kiribati and Tuvalu may find themselves completely under water by the end of this century. The inhabitants of these nations blame the developed world for emitting the **greenhouse gases** and **carbon dioxide** that are warming the planet, melting ice, and raising sea levels.

Text-Dependent Questions

1. What are the foundations of well-being?
2. Why is access to information still low in countries such as China, Myanmar, and all the island nations of the Pacific?
3. What is biodiversity?

Research Projects

Are the Pacific island nations really in danger of disappearing beneath the Pacific Ocean? Why? What steps are island nations and the rest of the world taking to prevent this from happening or to take care of island residents if it does?

Muslim Uighurs riot in China's Xinjiang region, where tensions have long simmered amid Uighur claims of repression.

CHAPTER 3

OPPORTUNITY

Words to Understand

Contraception: any form of birth control used to prevent pregnancy.

Corruption: the dishonest behavior by people in positions of power for their own benefit.

Junta: a totalitarian military government that takes power by force and uses military strength to enforce its rule.

Indigenous people: groups of culturally distinct groups with long-standing ties to the land in a specific area.

IUD: intrauterine device, a small device inserted into the uterus to prevent pregnancy.

Prejudice: an opinion that isn't based on facts or reason.

Stereotypes: a common belief about the nature of the members of a specific group that is based on limited experience or incorrect information.

Tertiary education: education that follows secondary education (high school), such as college.

Transparency: the government operates in a way that is visible to and understood by the public.

*O*pportunity is a person's ability to improve his or her life and simply to live it without interference. Opportunity comes from personal freedom and education. It can be hampered by intolerance, **prejudice**, or simple lack of access to colleges and universities.

To measure opportunity worldwide, the Social Progress Imperative scored countries in the following categories:

Personal Rights: *Are people's individual rights restricted by the government?*

Personal Freedom and Choice: *Are people allowed to make their own decisions?*

Tolerance and Inclusion: *Does everyone have the same opportunity to contribute?*

Access to Advanced Education: *Does everyone have the opportunity to go to college?*

Some countries of the East Asia Pacific region do very well in this area. As expected, New Zealand and Australia score among the best nations in the world, ranking second and third overall. (Canada gets first place.) Japan does very well in Personal Rights with room for improvement in Tolerance and Inclusion. Mongolia, South Korea, and the Philippines do not do badly overall. Other East Asian countries, however, have fairly disastrous scores in this area. Myanmar, China, Laos, and Cambodia all are in the bottom of the Opportunity rankings. Vietnam is not ranked but receives a dismal score of 36.28, which puts it between China (110th) and Myanmar (123rd).

Personal Rights

Personal rights are political and economic freedoms. They include the right to give your opinion without going to prison, to go wherever you want whenever you want, and to own your own property. The US Constitution, for example, protects several personal rights. Citizens are guaranteed the right to free speech, a free press, and freedom of association (that is, the right to join groups or political parties). These rights exist in some East Asia Pacific nations as well, but definitely not in all of them.

Antigovernment protesters clash with police outside a government ministry in Bangkok, Thailand. Protesters rallied against elections and called for political reform.

New Zealand and Australia take first and second place for protecting full personal rights, with Japan right behind at fifth place. Mongolia, South Korea, and the Philippines do not do too badly either. But the East Asia Pacific region has its fair share of repressive governments. Vietnam, Cambodia, China, and Myanmar are notorious for preventing citizens from living as they wish.

Myanmar's repressive government

Myanmar has long been a poster child for a repressive government. The nation was governed by a military **junta** for half of the 20th century and only formed a civilian government in 2011. The government was infamous for imprisoning political protesters; opposition leader and Nobel Peace Prize winner Aung San Suu Kyi spent most of the years between 1989 and 2010 under house arrest. The military was notorious for kidnapping children and forcing them to fight as soldiers. Several hundred thousand people of all ages were used as forced

NLD party campaign vehicle of Aung San Suu Kyi supports voter turnout in Bago, Myanmar.

labor, essentially as slaves. The government controls most newspapers and other publications and censors them heavily.

Myanmar's new civilian government promised to change things and passed a peaceful assembly law that allowed public protests, although as of 2015 police were still arresting protesters, and political party candidates were still being discouraged from speaking to journalists. The national election in the fall of 2015, the country's first free election in 25 years, resulted in the National League for Democracy, the party headed by Suu Kyi, winning a majority of seats in the 664-member parliament.

North Korean prison camps

When it comes to repression, North Korea is in a league of its own. Freedom of speech, assembly, and movement and private property rights are all severely limited, and citizens are expected to speak well of the government, no matter how badly it serves them. The government runs prison camps, where it imprisons people who speak out against the regime, try to find food for their families, or attempt to sneak across the border into China. They may stay in prison for years, working as slave labor in coal mines and being brainwashed with government propaganda. Prisoners are beaten, starved, and tortured. Prisoners get so hungry that they dig for worms in the soil. At the beginning of 2015, four camps were still open; US and South Korean officials estimated that they contained between 80,000 and 120,000 prisoners. The government continued to deny that the camps existed, though a North Korean diplomat admitted in 2014 that the nation did operate "reform through labor" centers. For the Human Righs Watch Report on North Korea, visit https://www.hrw.org/world-report/2015/country-chapters/north-korea.

Personal Freedom and Choice

The category Personal Freedom and Choice includes personal decisions, such as how to spend one's life, which religion to practice, freedom to marry or not, and freedom to control how many children one has. These rights exist in much of the East Asia Pacific region, but they are definitely curtailed in certain places.

The category also includes measures of governmental **corruption**; a corrupt and dishonest government is unpredictable and makes it impossible for people to plan their lives. Most East Asian nations do either well or moderately

More than 200,000 Malaysians join in peaceful protest for clean government in Kuala Lumpur, Malaysia, organized by the pro-democracy group Bersih (Malay for "clean").

well in this area. New Zealand ranks second for the world's lowest level of governmental corruption. Japan, South Korea, and Malaysia also shine in this category. Myanmar, however, ranked 126th in this category, has one of the most corrupt governments in the world. **Transparency**, the government's operating in a way that people can see and criticize, has been virtually nonexistent in Myanmar; citizens are hopeful that the situation will improve following the elections of 2015.

Contraception and population growth

Access to **contraception**, or birth control, is essential to scheduling one's life. Both men and women need to be able to decide when they will have children, with whom, and how many children they will have. Uncontrolled pregnancies can prevent women from studying, working, and thereby improving their own lives and those of their children. Controlling births also helps the society avoid rapid population growth, which causes significant problems, including lack of educational services and lack of opportunities for young people.

In most of the developed portions of the East Asia Pacific region, access to contraception is taken for granted. Women can take birth control pills, get shots, use intrauterine devices (**IUDs**), or be surgically sterilized; men can buy condoms, which also prevent the spread of HIV. This is not the case everywhere, however.

In Cambodia and Laos, only about 50 percent of people regularly use contraception. Both of these nations also have fairly high infant mortality rates, which somewhat counteracts the population growth caused by a high birth rate. Contraception is rare in a number of Pacific islands, and their populations are growing rapidly. In the Solomon Islands, 34 percent of people use contraceptives. Each woman bears an average of 3.28 children, putting the population growth rate at 2 percent, one of the faster rates worldwide. Timor-Leste has a very low contraception rate, just 22 percent in 2009–2010. The average woman there bears 5.0 children, giving Timor-Leste a population growth rate of 2.42 percent—30th in the world in 2015.

One-Child China

China is known for being one of the more repressive regimes in Asia, ranked a dismal 132nd for personal rights. The government restricts freedom of speech and of the press. Political protests are often shut down quickly and protesters can be thrown in prison. And although the SPI ranks China a decent 40 in Personal Freedom and Choice, for 35 years one of China's best-known restrictions on personal freedom was its strict one-child policy—a policy just ended in 2015.

In 1980, worried that China's population was growing too rapidly, the government passed a law prohibiting couples from having more than one child. Couples that violated the law lost benefits that helped with childcare and education. Some women were forced to have abortions, be surgically sterilized, or have IUDs inserted to prevent further pregnancies.

The one-child policy made China's current population disproportionately male; couples preferred to have boys because elderly parents traditionally live with their sons, so some chose to abort female fetuses. This has made it impossible for many young men to find wives, and has caused the fertility rate to drop precipitously, which could trigger economic crises in the future. Concerned with maintaining economic growth, in 2015 the government abruptly scrapped the one-child policy. Couples are now allowed to have two children. The new policy met with some enthusiasm but also considerable dismay from people who had missed their chance to have a second child.

Tolerance and Inclusion

In a society, do **stereotypes** and prejudices play a large role in access to education, jobs, and other opportunities? Are people prevented from contributing to the society because of their race, religion, or national origin? They are in many places.

Prejudices against indigenous peoples

In China (ranked 111th), an **indigenous people** called the Uighur live in Xinjiang, in the west of the country. Uighurs are Muslims, ethnically part of the Turkic group, which includes Turks. Ethnic Chinese people have moved into the area and taken advantage of the region's oil and mineral wealth, displacing the native Uighurs, who experience high unemployment. The Uighurs suffer considerable racial prejudice. They are not allowed to stay in hotels in China, for example, and complain that they are mistreated by Chinese police, though the Chinese government reports that it is only trying to suppress violence by Islamic extremists.

Myanmar's government (ranked 124th) is particularly harsh to a group of people called the Rohingya, a Muslim minority that many Burmese claim are illegal immigrants and whom the government refuses to recognize as citizens. The Rohingya have now become targets for human traffickers, who abuse them and use them as forced labor.

Burmese Rohingya Association members protesting as part of World Refugee Rally in Brisbane, Australia.

The most tolerant nations

Australia is a standout in the area of tolerance and inclusion; it ranks 11th in the world. Most Australians accept racial and cultural differences. Australia is multicultural. Half of Australians were born in another country or had at least one parent born overseas. Nearly 7 million immigrants have settled there since 1945, and Australia continues to welcome new immigrants. Although the original settlers were British and Irish, today large numbers come from India,

China, and South Africa, as well as neighboring New Zealand. Australia has accepted refugees from countries such as Vietnam, the former Soviet Union, Iraq, and the former Yugoslav republics. Australian law prevents discrimination on the basis of nationality, gender, age, or religious beliefs.

New Zealand wins even higher marks for tolerance, fifth best in the world. The nation is committed to religious freedom. One out of eight New Zealanders is of Asian descent, and although English is still the predominant language, there are many speakers of Maori, Samoan, and Hindi. Over the past decade the number of New Zealanders who identify themselves as Christian has dropped, while the number of Hindus, Muslims, and Buddhists has increased substantially. Even tolerant New Zealand, though, has seen an increase in reported instances of discrimination against Muslims.

Access to Advanced Education

Advanced education, or tertiary schooling, is essential to advancing a nation's overall economy. Without higher education, most jobs will remain low-skilled, and a nation will not be able to attract high-tech industries. There is uneven access to advanced education throughout the region. China is strong in globally ranked universities but suffers because fewer women earn higher degrees. Indonesia also has good universities. South Korea stands out in keeping women in school and overall providing education after high school. Cambodia, Laos, Timor-Leste, and Vietnam rank very poorly in this area. Through the rest of East Asia, **tertiary education** is the exception rather than the rule. Higher education of women is particularly low in Cambodia and Laos.

The Japanese University Game

Education in Japan is serious business. Competition for the top universities is fierce. Japanese universities select their students on the basis of admissions exams administered once a year; high school grades and activities are not considered important. Preparation for these exams starts years ahead of time, sometimes as early as first grade.

The Japanese K–12 grade arrangement resembles the American system of the mid-20th century. Six years of elementary school are followed by three years of junior high school (7th through 9th grades) and three years of either academic or vocational senior high school (10th through 12th grades). But school alone is not enough to ensure admission to a good university. Students of all ages attend evening schools called *juku*, where they take extra lessons in important subjects in addition to their regular daytime schoolwork. The pressure increases through high school. School pressure has even been identified as a factor in the country's high suicide rate. Serious high school students have no time for friends, activities, or even sleep. They just study. Students who fail to pass the tests for their chosen universities may take a year off to devote themselves to full-time studying, hoping for a better outcome when they try again.

Once a student enters college, though, life changes completely. Japanese university students are notorious for skipping class and having a good time. Nevertheless, they must find some time to study because Japanese universities are ranked among the best in the world.

Text-Dependent Questions

1. What are personal rights?
2. What policy did China adopt in 1980 to head off uncontrolled population growth? What were the consequences?
3. How do students get into universities in Japan?

Research Projects

Choose any country in the East Asia Pacific region and research its history, focusing particularly on the 19th and 20th centuries. How has this nation's history affected its attitudes toward tolerance and inclusion and personal freedoms?

A container ship in Shanghai, China, takes on freight bound for Hamburg, Germany.

CHAPTER 4

EAST ASIAN AND PACIFIC COUNTRIES AT A GLANCE

AUSTRALIA

QUICK STATS
Population: 22,751,014
Urban Population: 89.4% of population
Comparative Size: slightly smaller than US contiguous 48 states
Gross Domestic Product (per capita): $46,400 (24th worldwide)
Gross Domestic Product (by sector): agriculture 3.7%, industry 28.9%, services 67.4%
Government: federal parliamentary democracy and a Commonwealth realm
Language: English

SOCIAL PROGRESS SNAPSHOT
Social Progress Index: 86.42 (+25.42 above 61 world average)
Basic Human Needs: 93.73 (+25.40 above 68.33 world average)
Foundations of Well-being: 79.98 (+13.53 above 66.45 world average)
Opportunity: 85.55 (+37.32 above 48.23 world average)

Prehistoric settlers arrived on Australia from Southeast Asia at least 40,000 years ago, and their descendants remain. All of Australia was claimed as British territory in 1829. The nation became the Commonwealth of Australia in 1901. In recent decades Australia has become an internationally competitive, advanced market economy. The driest inhabited continent on earth, Australia is home to 10 percent of the world's biodiversity and many plants and animals that exist nowhere else in the world.

Aborigines, or indigenous people, in Northern Territory, Australia.

Follow the index every year at socialprogressimperative.org.
Quick Stats from CIA World Factbook.

EAST ASIAN AND PACIFIC COUNTRIES AT A GLANCE   61

A visitor reposes at Bayon Wat, part of a Buddhist temple complex built at the heart of the Khmer kingdom from the ninth to twelfth centuries.

CAMBODIA

QUICK STATS

Population: 15,708,756
Urban Population: 20.7% of population
Comparative Size: slightly smaller than Oklahoma
Gross Domestic Product (per capita): $3,300 (183rd worldwide)
Gross Domestic Product (by sector): agriculture 32.7%, industry 25.5%, services 41.8%
Government: multiparty democracy under a constitutional monarchy
Language: Khmer (official)

SOCIAL PROGRESS SNAPSHOT

Social Progress Index: 53.96 (–7.04 below 61 world average)
Basic Human Needs: 53.86 (–14.47 below 68.33 world average)
Foundations of Well-being: 67.52 (+1.07 above 66.45 world average)
Opportunity: 40.52 (–7.71 below 48.23 world average)

After centuries of domination by France, Japan, and the repressive Khmer Rouge regime of the 1970s, Cambodia remains one of the poorest countries in Asia. In 2012 approximately 2.66 million people lived on less than $1.20 per day, and 37 percent of Cambodian children under the age of 5 suffered from chronic malnutrition. More than 50 percent of the population is less than 25 years old. The population lacks education and productive skills, particularly in the impoverished countryside, which also lacks basic infrastructure.

CHINA

QUICK STATS

Population: 1,367,485,388
Urban Population: 55.6% of population
Comparative Size: slightly smaller than the United States
Gross Domestic Product (per capita): $12,900 (113th worldwide)
Gross Domestic Product (by sector): agriculture 9.2%, industry 42.6%, services 48.2%
Government: Communist state
Languages: Standard Chinese or Mandarin (official; Putonghua, based on the Beijing dialect), Yue (Cantonese), Wu (Shanghainese), Minbei (Fuzhou), Minnan (Hokkien-Taiwanese), Xiang, Gan, Hakka dialects, minority languages

SOCIAL PROGRESS SNAPSHOT

Social Progress Index: 59.07 (–1.93 below 61 world average)
Basic Human Needs: 73.74 (+5.41 above 68.33 world average)
Foundations of Well-being: 65.40 (–1.05 below 66.45 world average)
Opportunity: 38.08 (–10.15 below 48.23 world average)

For centuries China stood as a leading civilization, outpacing the rest of the world in the arts and sciences. A Communist government established after World War II imposed strict controls over everyday life and cost the lives of tens of millions of people. China has worked on developing its market economy since 1978, urbanizing rapidly, improving living standards, and allowing more personal choice. The Chinese government still faces numerous economic challenges, including creating more jobs for a growing middle class, persuading people to spend more and save less, reducing corruption, and slowing the serious environmental damage and pollution that have been the norm for the past decades.

INDONESIA

QUICK STATS

Population: 255,993,674
Urban Population: 53.7% of population
Comparative Size: slightly less than three times the size of Texas
Gross Domestic Product (per capita): $10,600 (133rd worldwide)
Gross Domestic Product (by sector): agriculture 14.2%, industry 45.5%, services 40.3%
Government: republic
Languages: Bahasa Indonesia (official, modified form of Malay), English, Dutch, local dialects (of which the most widely spoken is Javanese); more than 700 languages are used in Indonesia

SOCIAL PROGRESS SNAPSHOT

Social Progress Index: 60.47 (–0.53 below 61 world average)
Basic Human Needs: 66.52 (–1.81 below 68.33 world average)
Foundations of Well-being: 69.54 (+3.09 above 66.45 world average)
Opportunity: 45.35 (–2.88 below 48.23 world average)

The Dutch colonized Indonesia in the early 17th century. The nation became independent in 1949 and suffered several decades of government instability, authoritarian rule, coups, and periodic martial law. In 1999 Indonesia held free and fair legislative elections and since then has been fairly peaceful, although it continues to experience conflict with separatist groups. Indonesia is now the world's third most populous democracy, the world's largest archipelagic state, and the world's largest Muslim-majority nation. It is still troubled with poverty, infectious diseases, lack of education, terrorism, corruption in the government and the criminal justice system, and human rights violations by the police and the military.

JAPAN

QUICK STATS

Population: 126,919,659
Urban Population: 93.5% of population
Comparative Size: slightly smaller than California
Gross Domestic Product (per capita): $37,400 (43rd worldwide)
Gross Domestic Product (by sector): agriculture 1.2%, industry 24.5%, services 74.3%
Government: parliamentary government with a constitutional monarchy
Language: Japanese

SOCIAL PROGRESS SNAPSHOT

Social Progress Index: 83.15 (+22.15 above 61 world average)
Basic Human Needs: 95.01 (+26.68 above 68.33 world average)
Foundations of Well-being: 78.78 (+12.33 above 66.45 world average)
Opportunity: 75.66 (+27.43 above 48.23 world average)

After its defeat in World War II, Japan recovered to become an economic power and an ally of the United States. While the emperor retains his throne as a symbol of national unity, elected politicians hold actual decision-making power. Following three decades of unprecedented growth, Japan's economy experienced a major slowdown starting in the 1990s, but the country remains an economic power. Today Japan is among the world's largest and most technologically advanced economies.

KOREA, NORTH (DEMOCRATIC PEOPLE'S REPUBLIC OF KOREA)

QUICK STATS

Population: 24,983,205
Urban Population: 60.9% of total population
Comparative Size: slightly larger than Virginia; slightly smaller than Mississippi
Gross Domestic Product (per capita): $1,800 (209th worldwide)
Gross Domestic Product (by sector): agriculture 22%, industry 47%, services 31%
Government: Communist state one-man dictatorship
Languages: Korean

SOCIAL PROGRESS SNAPSHOT

(Scores not computed due to gaps in statistical sources)

An independent kingdom for much of its long history, Korea was occupied by Japan beginning in 1905 following the Russo-Japanese War. Five years later, Japan formally annexed the entire peninsula. Following World War II, Korea was split with the northern half coming under Soviet-sponsored Communist control. After failing in the Korean War (1950-53) to conquer the US-backed Republic of Korea (ROK) in the southern portion by force, North Korea (DPRK), under its founder President Kim Il Sung, adopted a policy of ostensible diplomatic and economic "self-reliance" as a check against outside influence.

North Korea, one of the world's most centrally directed and least open economies, faces chronic economic problems. Large-scale military spending draws off resources needed for investment and civilian consumption. North Korea has no independent media, and televisions are pre-tuned to government stations.

KOREA, SOUTH (REPUBLIC OF)

QUICK STATS

Population: 49,115,196
Urban Population: 82.5% of population
Comparative Size: slightly smaller than Pennsylvania; slightly larger than Indiana
Gross Domestic Product (per capita): $35,300 (46th worldwide)
Gross Domestic Product (by sector): agriculture 2.3%, industry 38.3%, services 59.4%
Government: republic
Languages: Korean, English (widely taught in junior high and high school)

SOCIAL PROGRESS SNAPSHOT

Social Progress Index: 77.70 (+16.70 above 61 world average)
Basic Human Needs: 89.11 (+20.78 above 68.33 world average)
Foundations of Well-being: 75.60 (+9.15 above 66.45 world average)
Opportunity: 68.40 (+20.17 above 48.23 world average)

Korea split in two after World War II. South Korea (Republic of Korea, ROK) formed a democratic government. A Communist-style government was installed in North Korea (Democratic People's Republic of Korea, DPRK). The 1953 armistice split the peninsula along a demilitarized zone at about the 38th parallel, and the two nations are continually at odds. South Korea over the past four decades has demonstrated incredible economic growth and global integration to become a high-tech industrialized economy.

LAOS

QUICK STATS

Population: 6,911,544
Urban Population: 38.6% of population
Comparative Size: slightly larger than Utah
Gross Domestic Product (per capita): $5,000 (167th worldwide)
Gross Domestic Product (by sector): agriculture 23.7%, industry 32.2%, services 44.1%
Government: Communist state
Languages: Lao (official), French, English, various ethnic languages

SOCIAL PROGRESS SNAPSHOT

Social Progress Index: 52.41 (–8.59 below 61 world average)
Basic Human Needs: 60.43 (–7.90 below 68.33 world average)
Foundations of Well-being: 61.70 (–4.75 below 66.45 world average)
Opportunity: 35.09 (–13.14 below 48.23 world average)

The government of Laos, one of the few remaining one-party Communist states, began decentralizing control and encouraging private enterprise in 1986. The country's growth has been among the fastest in Asia. Nevertheless, its infrastructure remains undeveloped, with a very basic road system and limited external and internal landline telecommunications. The government appears committed to raising the country's profile among foreign investors, but Laos lacks both skilled and unskilled workers to attract investment.

Kampung Bako is a small fishing community in Sarawak, Borneo, an island shared by Malaysia, Singapore, and Indonesia. Local people belong to the Bidayuh tribe of Dayaks and make their living from fishing and tourism. Kampung Bako is in Malaysia.

MALAYSIA

QUICK STATS

Population: 30,513,848
Urban Population: 74.7% of population
Comparative Size: slightly larger than New Mexico
Gross Domestic Product (per capita): $24,700 (71st worldwide)
Gross Domestic Product (by sector): agriculture 9.3%, industry 34.7%, services 56%
Government: constitutional monarchy
Languages: Bahasa Malaysia (official), English, Chinese (Cantonese, Mandarin, Hokkien, Hakka, Hainan, Foochow), Tamil, Telugu, Malayalam, Panjabi, Thai; several indigenous languages

SOCIAL PROGRESS SNAPSHOT

Social Progress Index: 69.55 (+8.55 above 61 world average)
Basic Human Needs: 86.13 (+17.80 above 68.33 world average)
Foundations of Well-being: 74.87 (+8.42 above 66.45 world average)
Opportunity: 47.66 (–0.57 below 48.23 world average)

Malaysia was formed in 1963 from the former British-ruled territories on the Malay peninsula and Sabah and Sarawak in Borneo. Malaysia, a middle-income country, has transformed itself since the 1970s from a producer of raw materials into an emerging multisector economy. Exports of electronics, oil and gas, palm oil, and rubber drive the economy. The oil and gas sector supplied about 29 percent of government revenue in 2014.

MONGOLIA

QUICK STATS

Population: 2,992,908
Urban Population: 72% of population
Comparative Size: slightly smaller than Alaska; more than twice the size of Texas
Gross Domestic Product (per capita): $11,900 (132nd worldwide)
Gross Domestic Product (by sector): agriculture 12.2%, industry 35%, services 52.8%
Government: parliamentary
Languages: Khalkha Mongol 90% (official), Turkic, Russian

SOCIAL PROGRESS SNAPSHOT

Social Progress Index: 61.52 (+0.52 above 61 world average)
Basic Human Needs: 58.36 (–9.97 below 68.33 world average)
Foundations of Well-being: 64.49 (–1.96 below 66.45 world average)
Opportunity: 61.71 (+13.48 above 48.23 world average)

Mongolia won its independence from China in 1921 with Soviet backing, and a Communist regime was installed in 1924. Following a peaceful democratic revolution in 1990, the ex-Communist Mongolian People's Revolutionary Party (MPRP) won most parliamentary elections and stayed in power either governing alone or in coalition into the 2010s. Mongolia's extensive mineral deposits and growth in mining-sector activities have transformed its economy, which traditionally has depended on herding and agriculture.

MYANMAR (BURMA)

QUICK STATS

Population: 56,320,206
Urban Population: 34.1% of population
Comparative Size: slightly smaller than Texas
Gross Domestic Product (per capita): $4,700 (170th worldwide)
Gross Domestic Product (by sector): agriculture 37.1%, industry 21.3%, services 41.6%
Government: parliamentary government took power in March 2011
Language: Burmese (official)

SOCIAL PROGRESS SNAPSHOT

Social Progress Index: 46.12 (–14.88 below 61 world average)
Basic Human Needs: 58.87 (–9.46 below 68.33 world average)
Foundations of Well-being: 49.19 (–17.26 below 66.45 world average)
Opportunity: 30.28 (–17.95 below 48.23 world average)

Myanmar (formerly Burma) was part of the British empire until 1948. After years of dominance by a brutal military junta that kept it isolated from the world, Myanmar held free elections in 2008 and established a civilian government in 2011. Since then, the government has made an effort to reform the nation and to open its closed borders. Most of the world has referred to the nation as Myanmar since the military government adopted that name in 1988. The residents of the nation themselves have used both terms for centuries; Burma is the spoken name, and Myanmar is a formal word used in writing.

Thousands rally for action on climate change around New Zealand. The golden toad is the first species to go extinct due to climate change.

NEW ZEALAND

QUICK STATS

Population: 4,438,393
Urban Population: 86.3% of population
Comparative Size: almost twice the size of North Carolina; about the size of Colorado
Gross Domestic Product (per capita): $35,200 (47th worldwide)
Gross Domestic Product (by sector): agriculture 3.8%, industry 26.6%, services 69.9%
Government: parliamentary democracy and a Commonwealth realm
Languages: English (official) 89.8%, Maori (official) 3.5%, Samoan 2%, Hindi 1.6%, French 1.2%, Northern Chinese 1.2%, Yue 1%, other or not stated 20.5%, New Zealand Sign Language (official)

SOCIAL PROGRESS SNAPSHOT

Social Progress Index: 87.08 (+26.08 above 61 world average)
Basic Human Needs: 92.87 (+24.54 above 68.33 world average)
Foundations of Well-being: 82.77 (+16.32 above 66.45 world average)
Opportunity: 85.61 (+37.38 above 48.23 world average)

The Polynesian Maori reached New Zealand in about AD 800. In 1840 their chieftains entered into an agreement with Britain, the Treaty of Waitangi, in which they ceded sovereignty to Queen Victoria while retaining territorial rights. The British colony of New Zealand became an independent dominion in 1907 and supported Great Britain militarily in both world wars. In recent years the government has sought to address long-standing Maori grievances. Over the past 30 years the government has transformed New Zealand from an agrarian economy dependent on British market access to a more industrialized, free market economy that can compete globally.

PAPUA NEW GUINEA

QUICK STATS
Population: 6,672,429
Urban Population: 13% of population
Comparative Size: slightly larger than California
Gross Domestic Product (per capita): $2,400 (198th worldwide)
Gross Domestic Product (by sector): agriculture 26.3%, industry 39%, services 34.8%
Government: constitutional parliamentary democracy and a Commonwealth realm
Languages: Tok Pisin (official), English (official), Hiri Motu (official), some 836 indigenous languages spoken (about 12% of the world's total); most languages have fewer than 1,000 speakers

SOCIAL PROGRESS SNAPSHOT
Foundations of Well-being: 55.39 (–11.06 below 66.45 world average)
(Not all scores computed due to data gaps in statistical sources.)

The eastern half of the island of New Guinea was divided between Germany (north) and Great Britain (south) in 1885. The south was transferred to Australia in 1902, which occupied the northern portion during World War I and continued to administer the combined areas until independence in 1975. Papua New Guinea has many natural resources, particularly minerals such as copper, gold, and oil, but it is hard to reach them due to rugged terrain, land ownership issues, and the high cost of developing infrastructure. The formal economy is very small and focused mainly on the export of those natural resources. An estimated 85 percent of the population are subsistence farmers.

PHILIPPINES

QUICK STATS
Population: 100,998,376
Urban Population: 44.4% of population
Comparative Size: slightly less than twice the size of Georgia; slightly larger than Arizona
Gross Domestic Product (per capita): $7,000 (60th worldwide)
Gross Domestic Product (by sector): agriculture 11.3%, industry 31.2%, services 57.4%
Government: republic
Languages: Filipino (official; based on Tagalog) and English (official); eight major dialects: Tagalog, Cebuano, Ilocano, Hiligaynon or Ilonggo, Bicol, Waray, Pampango, and Pangasinan

SOCIAL PROGRESS SNAPSHOT
Social Progress Index: 65.46 (+4.46 above world average)
Basic Human Needs: 68.23 (–0.10 below 68.33 world average)
Foundations of Well-being: 68.86 (+2.41 above 66.45 world average)
Opportunity: 59.30 (+11.07 above 48.23 world average)

The Republic of the Philippines attained its independence in July 1946. Rule since then has been hampered by lengthy dictatorships, several attempted coups, government instability, and conflict with China over disputed territorial and maritime claims in the South China Sea. Infrastructure remains underfunded, and the government is relying on the private sector to help with major projects under its Public-Private Partnership program. Other long-term challenges are reforming governance, the judicial system, and the regulatory environment and improving the ease of doing business.

Singapore—Locals, expats (for expatriates, or people who live in a country other than where they grew up), and tourists enjoy the warm night air beside the Singapore River overlooked by the colorful neon bars and al fresco restaurants of Clarke Quay in Kampong Malacca.

SINGAPORE

QUICK STATS

Population: 5,674,472
Urban Population: 100% of population
Comparative Size: slightly more than 3.5 times the size of Washington, DC
Gross Domestic Product (per capita): $82,800 (7th worldwide)
Gross Domestic Product (by sector): agriculture 0%, industry 25%, services 75%
Government: parliamentary republic
Languages: Mandarin (official) 36.3%, English (official) 29.8%, Malay (official) 11.9%, Hokkien 8.1%, Tamil (official) 4.4%, Cantonese 4.1%, Teochew 3.2%, other Indian languages 1.2%, other Chinese dialects 1.1%, other 1.1%

SOCIAL PROGRESS SNAPSHOT

Opportunity: 62.83 (+14.60 above 48.23 world average)
(Not all scores computed due to data gaps in statistical sources.)

Singapore was founded as a British trading colony in 1819. It joined the Malaysian Federation in 1963 but was ousted two years later and became independent. Singapore is now one of the world's most prosperous countries, with strong international trading links (its port is one of the world's busiest in terms of tonnage handled) and with per capita GDP equal to that of the leading nations of Western Europe. Singapore has a highly developed and successful free market economy. It enjoys a remarkably open and corruption-free environment, stable prices, and low unemployment.

THAILAND

QUICK STATS

Population: 67,976,405
Urban Population: 50.4% of population
Comparative Size: about three times the size of Florida; slightly more than twice the size of Wyoming
Gross Domestic Product (per capita): $14,400 (106th worldwide)
Gross Domestic Product (by sector): agriculture 11.6%, industry 32.6%, services 55.8%
Government: constitutional monarchy
Languages: Thai (official) 90.7%, Burmese 1.3%, other 8%

SOCIAL PROGRESS SNAPSHOT

Social Progress Index: 66.34 (+5.34 above 61 world average)
Basic Human Needs: 75.77 (+7.44 above 68.33 world average)
Foundations of Well-being: 72.35 (+5.90 above 66.45 world average)
Opportunity: 50.90 (+2.67 above 48.23 world average)

Known as Siam until 1939, Thailand is the only Southeast Asian country never to have been colonized by a European power. A bloodless revolution in 1932 led to the establishment of a constitutional monarchy. In alliance with Japan during World War II, Thailand became a US treaty ally in 1954 after sending troops to Korea and later fighting alongside the United States in Vietnam. Since 2005 Thailand has experienced several rounds of political turmoil. With a well-developed infrastructure and generally pro-investment policies, Thailand has historically had a strong economy.

TIMOR-LESTE

QUICK STATS

Population: 1,231,116
Urban Population: 32.8% of population
Comparative Size: slightly larger than Connecticut
Gross Domestic Product (per capita): $4,900 (155th worldwide)
Gross Domestic Product (by sector): agriculture 5.2%, industry 72.8%, services 22.1%
Government: republic
Languages: Tetum (official), Portuguese (official), Indonesian, English. There are about 16 indigenous languages; Tetum, Galole, Mambae, and Kemak are spoken by a significant portion of the population.

SOCIAL PROGRESS SNAPSHOT

Basic Human Needs: 50.55 (−17.78 below 68.33 world average)
Foundations of Well-being: 59.34 (−7.11 below 66.45 world average)
(Not all scores computed due to data gaps in statistical sources.)

Timor-Leste (formerly East Timor), one of the newest nations in the world, became an independent state in 2002. The island state has been plagued with violence and instability since its origin. Timor-Leste faces great challenges in rebuilding its infrastructure, strengthening the civil administration, and generating jobs for young people entering the workforce. The development of oil and gas resources in offshore waters has greatly supplemented government revenues.

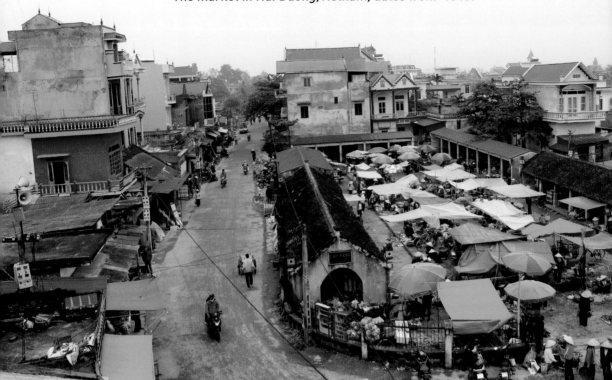

The market in Hai Duong, Vietnam, dates from 1845.

VIETNAM

QUICK STATS

Population: 94,348,835
Urban Population: 33.6% of population
Comparative Size: about three times the size of Tennessee; slightly larger than New Mexico
Gross Domestic Product (per capita): $5,600 (163rd worldwide)
Gross Domestic Product (by sector): agriculture17.9 %, industry 38.1%, services 44%
Government: Communist state
Languages: Vietnamese (official), English (increasingly favored as a second language), some French, Chinese, and Khmer, mountain-area languages (Mon-Khmer and Malayo-Polynesian)

SOCIAL PROGRESS SNAPSHOT

Basic Human Needs: 74.19 (+5.86 above 68.33 world average)
Opportunity: 36.28 (–11.95 below 48.23 world average)
(Not all scores computed due to data gaps in statistical sources.)

Vietnam became part of French Indochina in 1887. After Ho Chi Minh's Communist forces defeated France in 1954, Vietnam was divided into the Communist North and anti-Communist South. US economic and military aid to South Vietnam grew through the 1960s in an attempt to bolster the government, but US armed forces were withdrawn following a ceasefire agreement in 1973. Two years later North Vietnamese forces overran the South, reuniting the country under Communist rule. Since the enactment of Vietnam's *doi moi* (renovation) policy in 1986, Vietnamese authorities have worked to modernize the economy. The Communist leaders maintain tight control on political expression.

Conclusion

Although some of the nations of the East Asia Pacific region earn low scores in certain areas, for the most part the region has seen good social progress during the first years of the 21st century. More people have enough to eat. Education is more common. The so-called Four Asian Tigers—Hong Kong, Singapore, South Korea, and Taiwan—spent the end of the 20th century rapidly industrializing and are now advanced societies with strong economies. New Zealand and Australia are the highest-performing countries in the world in terms of overall social progress.

On the other hand, the Social Progress Imperative ranks several East Asian nations as low in terms of social progress. Cambodia, Laos, Myanmar, and Vietnam, like their neighbors Bangladesh and India, face serious challenges in development in several areas. The organization hopes that its assessments can identify the areas most in need of help, as well as possible role models.

Numerous agencies are working to help the nations that need improvement. The FAO keeps statistics and provides help on agriculture and food production, with an eye toward ensuring that all people have sufficient calories and nutrients for their daily energy needs. The World Health Organization (WHO) keeps track of mortality from infectious diseases; the region has seen real improvement in this area, particularly in mortality from malaria and diseases that can be prevented with vaccines, such as polio. The WHO and UNICEF offer aid to improve sanitation and plumbing. Other sources of information and aid are the Pew Research Center, the Gallup World Poll, Transparency International, the Organization for Economic Co-operation and Development (OECD), the

World Resources Institute, the United Nations Development Programme, and the World Bank. The Red Cross, Doctors Without Borders, UNICEF, and the World Bank's International Development Organization (IDO) are just a few of the organizations that work to help improve human lives worldwide. The IDO, for example, is funding projects to improve sanitation in Sri Lanka, build solar panels for irrigation in Bangladesh, and install electricity throughout rural Myanmar by 2030.

Can you do anything to help improve living conditions for people in other parts of the world? Yes, you can. The easiest thing to do is donate money to organizations that provide aid. If you would like to do more, there are various volunteer and paid opportunities available in many areas, such as teaching English or helping children with disabilities.

After college, the Peace Corps hires people for jobs that last from several months to two years. There are numerous other paid opportunities throughout the region. English-teaching jobs are almost always a possibility for native English speakers with college degrees, and learning English is one of the best ways for people to improve their prospects in life. Working in development will not make you rich, but it can be very satisfying and a real adventure.

In the meantime and at home, you can simply follow the news. Read about what is happening in Asia, the Pacific, and other continents as well. The world is interconnected now, and events on the far side of the globe can certainly affect your life.

Series Glossary

Anemia: a condition in which the blood doesn't have enough healthy red blood cells, most often caused by not having enough iron

Aquifer: an underground layer of water-bearing permeable rock, from which groundwater can be extracted using a water well

Asylum: protection granted by a nation to someone who has left their native country as a political refugee

Basic human needs: the things people need to stay alive: clean water, sanitation, food, shelter, basic medical care, safety

Biodiversity: the variety of life that is absolutely essential to the health of different ecosystems

Carbon dioxide (CO_2): a greenhouse gas that contributes to global warming and climate change

Censorship: the practice of officially examining books, movies, and other media and art, and suppressing unacceptable parts

Child mortality rate: the number of children that die before their fifth birthday for every 1,000 babies born alive

Contraception: any form of birth control used to prevent pregnancy

Corruption: the dishonest behavior by people in positions of power for their own benefit

Deforestation: the clearing of trees, transforming a forest into cleared land

Desalination: a process that removes minerals (including salt) from ocean water

Discrimination: the unjust or prejudicial treatment of different categories of people, especially on the grounds of race, age, or sex

Ecosystem: a biological community of interacting organisms and their physical environment

Ecosystem sustainability: when we care for resources like clean air, water, plants, and animals so that they will be available to future generations

Emissions: the production and discharge of something, especially gas or radiation

Ethnicities: social groups that have a common national or cultural tradition

Extremism: the holding of extreme political or religious views; fanaticism

Famine: a widespread scarcity of food that results in malnutrition and starvation on a large scale

Food desert: a neighborhood or community with no walking access to affordable, nutritious food

Food security: having enough to eat at all times

Greenhouse gas emissions: any of the atmospheric gases that contribute to the greenhouse effect by absorbing infrared radiation produced by solar warming of the earth's surface. They include carbon dioxide (CO_2), methane (CH_4), nitrous oxide (NO_2), and water vapor.

Gross domestic product (GDP): the total value of all products and services created in a country during a year

GDP per capita (per person): the gross domestic product divided by the number of people in the country. For example, if the GDP for a country is one hundred million dollars ($100,000,000) and the population is one million people (1,000,000), then the GDP per capita (value created per person) is $100.

Habitat: environment for a plant or animal, including climate, food, water, and shelter

Incarceration: the condition of being imprisoned

Income inequality: when the wealth of a country is spread very unevenly among the population

Indigenous people: culturally distinct groups with long-standing ties to the land in a specific area

Inflation: when the same amount money buys less from one day to the next. Just because things cost more does not mean that people have more money. Low-income people trapped in a high inflation economy can quickly find themselves unable to purchase even the basics like food.

Infrastructure: permanent features required for an economy to operate such as transportation routes and electric grids; also systems such as education and courts

Latrine: a communal outdoor toilet, such as a trench dug in the ground

Literate: able to read and write

Malnutrition: lack of proper nutrition, caused by not having enough to eat, not eating enough of the right things, or being unable to use the food that one does eat

Maternal mortality rate: the number of pregnant women who die for every 100,000 births.

Natural resources: industrial materials and assets provided by nature such as metal deposits, timber, and water

Nongovernmental organization (NGO): a nonprofit, voluntary citizens' group organized on a local, national, or international level. Examples include organizations that support human rights, advocate for political participation, and work for improved health care.

Parliament: a group of people who are responsible for making the laws in some kinds of government

Prejudice: an opinion that isn't based on facts or reason

Preventive care: health care that helps an individual avoid illness

Primary school: includes grades 1–6 (also known as elementary school); precedes **secondary** and **tertiary education**, schooling beyond the primary grades; secondary generally corresponds to high school, and tertiary generally means college-level

Privatization: the transfer of ownership, property, or business from the government to the private sector (the part of the national economy that is not under direct government control)

Sanitation: conditions relating to public health, especially the provision of clean drinking water and adequate sewage disposal

Stereotypes: are common beliefs about the nature of the members of a specific group that are based on limited experience or incorrect information

Subsistence agriculture: a system of farming that supplies the needs of the farm family without generating any surplus for sale

Surface water: the water found above ground in streams, lakes, and rivers

Tolerance: a fair, objective, and permissive attitude toward those whose opinions, beliefs, practices, racial or ethnic origins, and so on differ from one's own

Trafficking: dealing or trading in something illegal

Transparency: means that the government operates in a way that is visible to and understood by the public

Universal health care: a system in which every person in a country has access to doctors and hospitals

Urbanization: the process by which towns and cities are formed and become larger as more and more people begin living and working in central areas

Well-being: the feeling people have when they are healthy, comfortable, and happy

Whistleblower: someone who reveals private information about the illegal activities of a person or organization

Index

RESOURCES

Continue exploring the world of development through this assortment of online and print resources. Follow links, stay organized, and maintain a critical perspective. Also, seek out news sources from outside the country in which you live.

Websites

Social Progress Imperative: socialprogressimperative.org
United Nations—Human Development Indicators: hdr.undp.org/en/countries and Sustainable Development Goals: un.org/sustainabledevelopment/sustainable-development-goals
World Bank—World Development Indicators: data.worldbank.org/data-catalog/world-development-indicators
World Health Organization—country statistics: who.int/gho/countries/en
U.S. State Department—human rights tracking site: humanrights.gov/dyn/countries.html
Oxfam International: oxfam.org/en
Amnesty International: amnesty.org/en
Human Rights Watch: hrw.org
Reporters without Borders: en.rsf.org
CIA—The World Factbook: cia.gov/library/publications/the-world-factbook

Books

Literary and classics

The Good Earth, Pearl S. Buck
Grapes of Wrath, John Steinbeck
The Jungle, Upton Sinclair

Nonfiction—historical/classic

Angela's Ashes, Frank McCourt
Lakota Woman, Mary Crow Dog with Richard Erdoes
Orientalism, Edward Said
Silent Spring, Rachel Carson
The Souls of Black Folk, W.E.B. Du Bois

Nonfiction: development and policy—presenting a range of views

Behind the Beautiful Forevers: Life, Death, and Hope in a Mumbai Undercity, Katherine Boo
The Bottom Billion: Why the Poorest Countries Are Failing and What Can Be Done About It, Paul Collier
The End of Poverty, Jeffrey D. Sachs
For the Common Good: Redirecting the Economy toward Community, the Environment, and a Sustainable Future, Herman E. Daly
I Am Malala: The Girl Who Stood Up for Education and Was Shot by the Taliban, Malala Yousafzai and Christina Lamb
The Life You Can Save: Acting Now to End World Poverty, Peter Singer
Mismeasuring Our Lives: Why GDP Doesn't Add Up, Joseph E. Stiglitz, Amartya Sen, and Jean-Paul Fitoussi
Rachel and Her Children: Homeless Families in America, Jonathan Kozol
The White Man's Burden: Why the West's Efforts to Aid the Rest Have Done So Much Ill and So Little Good, William Easterly

Foreword writer Michael Green is an economist, author, and cofounder of the Social Progressive Imperative. A UK native and graduate of Oxford University, Green has worked in aid and development for the British government and taught economics at Warsaw University.

Author Amy Hackney Blackwell is a scientist with a law degree who has lived and worked around the world. She spent two years teaching in Japan, which was a perfect point from which to explore the whole Asia-Pacific region.